My First Leaf

Echoes of Love & Life

Gaganpreet Kaur

BookLeaf Publishing
India | USA | UK

Made with ❤ on the BookLeaf Publishing Platform
www.bookleafpub.in
www.bookleafpub.com

Dedication

To my dearest Mother and Father—
both devoted teachers—
whose belief in the power of words
and creativity
has always inspired me to write and
express myself freely.

Your encouragement, love, and lessons
have been the roots of my imagination.
This book is a tribute to the
foundation you've built within me.

Thank you for being my first mentors
and my forever guiding lights.

मैं सीख रही हूँ

माँ, मैं सीख रही हूँ
तुम-सी रोटी, तुम-सा खाना,
तुम जैसे भाग-भागकर काम निपटाना,

थोड़ी कच्ची हूँ , पर सीख जाऊँगी,
पर तुम-सी कभी न बन पाऊँगी।
चाहती हूँ कि मुझमें छवि तुम्हारी दिखे,
आख़िर तुमने ही तो मेरे जीवन के कुछ अद्‌भुत
अध्याय लिखे।

तुमसे सीखा आत्मनिर्भरता का ज्ञान,
तुम्हें शायद पता भी न होगा, माँ, कितना है तुमपर
मान।
मेरी शिक्षा के लिए तुम सबसे लड़ीं,तुम्हारी कोशिशों
से ही तो तुम्हारी ये बेटी पढ़ी।

आज भी याद है मुझे, मैं किताबें लेकर सो न जाऊँ,
इसलिए रात भर जागती थी तुम,
और अगर मैं सोती हुई पाई जाऊँ, तो कितनी निराश
हो जाती थीं तुम।

सच है माँ कि तूने मुझे बहुत कुछ दिया,
बस इस बात का मलाल है कि इस बेटी ने तेरे लिए कुछ न किया।
तेरे दिए पंख लगा के मैं इतनी दूर उड़ी,
अपने ख़्वाबों के पीछे इतनी तेज़ भागी कि वापस न मुड़ी।
मलाल है के, आज जब तू अकेले काम करती है,
मैं नहीं हूँ तेरे साथ हाथ बँटाने को,
रात में जब तेरे पैर दुखते हैं,
मैं नहीं हूँ उन पर गरम तेल लगाने को।

तबीयत ख़राब होती है तेरी जब,
हर बार तू मुझसे छुपाती है,
और जब मैं पूछती हूँ,
तो कहती है कि, “तुझे छुट्टी कब मिल पाती है?”
माँ, ये तेरी बेटी तुझ-सी बनना चाहती है,
तेरे जैसे समाज में सर उठाकर, अपनी शर्तों पर जीना चाहती है।

माँ, मैं सीख रही हूँ।तुझ-सी बनना सीख रही हूँ।

Acknowledgement

Heartfelt Gratitude for Loved Ones

As I reflect on the journey that led to this book, my heart is filled with deep gratitude for the remarkable individuals who have shaped my path.

To my parents, the foundation of my life: Your unwavering love, support, and guidance have been the pillars of every milestone I've reached. This book is a reflection of the values you instilled in me and the resilience you taught me to carry.

To my brother: Your calm presence, patience, and quiet encouragement have been a comfort in times of doubt. Thank you for always being there, in your own unique way.

To my husband: Your belief in me, even when I faltered, has been transformative. You have been my anchor, my encourager, and my greatest advocate. This book would not have been possible without your unwavering support.

To my friends and extended family: Your support, laughter, and encouragement have carried me through both the highs and the lows of this creative process. Your faith in me means more than words can express.

To my mentors and teachers: Thank you for sparking my curiosity and challenging me to think deeper. Your guidance helped me find and refine my voice.

And to you, dear reader: Thank you for choosing to spend your time with this book. I hope it speaks to your heart, offers comfort, and perhaps even a little courage.

This book is the culmination of countless late nights, persistent dreams, and the steady support of those who have walked alongside me. I dedicate it to all of you, with love and enduring gratitude.

Preface

Dear Reader,

My First Leaf is a journey through the intricate tapestry of the human experience, woven with threads of hope, resilience, and transformation. Within these pages, you'll find a collection of poems that reflect moments of personal evolution, heartfelt connection, and profound introspection.

The title, *My First Leaf*, symbolizes the beginning of a new chapter—much like the first leaf emerging from a budding tree—representing fresh starts and new perspectives.

Each poem in this collection is a testament to the strength found in vulnerability and the beauty that can arise from life's challenges.

In writing this book, I set out to capture the essence of navigating life's tumultuous waves with grace and courage.

From the trials of personal growth to the serenity found in love and self-discovery, these poems serve as a mirror reflecting a journey of learning, surviving, and evolving.

In the dance between light and shadow, joy and sorrow, growth and acceptance, I hope you'll find pieces of yourself mirrored in these words. May these reflections offer solace, inspiration, and a sense of shared experience.

Thank you for joining me on this poetic journey. It is my deepest hope that *My First Leaf* resonates with you, providing comfort and encouragement as we all continue to grow and thrive.

With gratitude and hope,
Gaganpreet Kaur

Art of Surviving

Yeah!! I learnt it, oh yeah!! I learnt it,
I have learnt the art of surviving.

The night was too cold and the darkness was deep,
But hurrah!!! I learnt it; I have learnt the art of existing.

My strength all gone, and buoyancy abated,
I was horrified and thought I would disintegrate,
That moment of weakness clouded my spine,
But then I heard a voice that said, "Don't worry, you'll be fine."

Go on, go on. You must not impede.
Hold your head high and proceed.
Determined, I decided to fight it out,
One step with nerve is what it's all about.

Doesn't matter if you're alone or unaided.
Gather all your freshness and strength that
faded.

Just one step forward, and I realised,
The sky gave me strength to walk and stay
alive.

Hold your head high,
Let's try to make it right.
Till I collapse, I will survive.

When I look at you.......

When I look at you,
It's your smile that brightens my day.
When I look at you,
All my worries and fears melt away.

When you're around, life feels pure and
whole.
When you're around, I feel a warm ecstasy in
my soul.

Your presence deeply affects my soul,
Transforming me—sheltered, poised, and
whole.

You are the force that carries me through,
My source of joy when I feel blue.

Your gaze so peaceful, your demeanour so rare,
I thank the force that brought you near.
I thank God for the blessing that is you,
For your warmth and love so true.
I thank Him for your shoulder—steadfast through thick and thin,
You by my side is my greatest win.

Be my strength and walk with me always.
For this beam on your face brightens my nights and adorns my days.

A letter to my parents

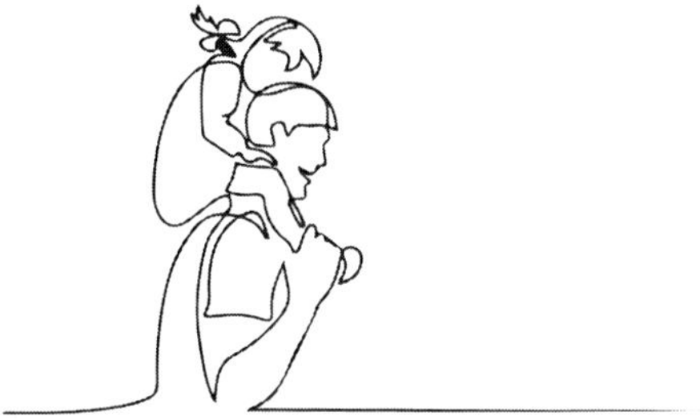

I start with the time when you were always near,
Home, my world—my priorities were crystal clear.
I saw the world through your loving gaze,
In my sheltered bubble, you were my guiding rays.

I am happy that I was the kind of toddler you always wanted.
I was your first child, so all my wishes were granted.

But I'm truly sorry, Dad, for the rebellious teenage years;
Mom, for the moments I brought you to tears.

Now, matured, I've ventured out on my own,
Facing solitude, sometimes feeling alone.

Mom, I miss your care when illness finds me,
Dad, your strength—I need it when darkness blinds me.

When life tests me, I shut my eyes tight,
Picture you both close, take a breath, find my light.

I know life might be easier if I stayed near you,
For no one else cares for me like you two.

I yearn to turn back time, to that little girl,
Safe in her shell, your precious pearl.

I wish I could get a piece of my childhood again,
Escape this chaos, this endless fight of loss and gain.

Even in distance, my heart holds you so dear,
I miss you profoundly, and I love you too.

Giving up..........

Giving up, letting go...
Was the most thorny task, so....
I decided to hold on,
Thinking, with time, the feeling of
abhorrence would be gone.

That wanting in my heart to see the karma
play its game,
Drenched the piety from my soul and filled it
with hatred I could never tame.

I look up to the sky and ask my holy Lord,
This is what I would turn out to be? I had
never thought.

Oh please! Oh please! Take this hatred away
And fill me back with virtue, I plea, I pray!!

I wish to be free,
Oh! Please help me be,
The person I always wanted to be.
A person who was always forgiving and
worthy.
Let it be... let me be free.

A Dream

On a dark, cozy night, beneath stars shining bright,
I glimpsed an image bathed in angelic light.
I was unaware—my attention slight,
As they approached quietly, their touch soft and white.

With simplicity and a gentle voice, they came near,
And as I drew closer, the shadows disappeared.
Bright light surrounded me, with wings of silver sheen —,
Their divine presence left me in awe, serene.

Confusion lingered, but one thing was clear:
I never wanted this vision to disappear.
In that moment, I kept my eyes closed tight,
For that dream brought me joy, and I wished
to hold it tight.

Through thick and thin

When I vow to stand by you through each rise and fall,
My promise remains steadfast—enduring through all..
I'll witness your hair embrace its silver hue,
With each passing day, my love, I'll cherish you.

We'll share countless debates and heartfelt talks,
Endless laughter and moonlit walks.
In cinema's glow and playful flirtations,
Our love will thrive through all life's variations.

Together, we'll greet countless sunsets, hand in hand,
As life unfolds—and we'll understand:
In our shared journey, there will be lessons to learn,
Yet our love will persist, forever bright and firm.

An Old Letter

I stumbled upon a letter from my past,
written when I was merely four,
Its innocence and candour hit me like a
breeze off the shore.

Scribbled words, not yet bound by language's
decree,
Yet the message to my Nana was as clear as
could be.

From unfiltered truths to less-than-flattering
art,
My paper creation expressed feelings from the
heart.

That letter revealed a truth I now recognize,
With age, the ability to speak openly often downsizes.

As adults, we grasp the language and its rules so tight,
Yet we also learn to veil our feelings, to make words sound right.

From that letter, I learned the beauty of honesty—,
And how, as we grow, we cloak our hearts in diplomacy.

In a race

Run and hustle, life's a race,
Hurry up and quicken your pace.
I know you wish you could slow down,
Savor the moment, take a look around..

Yet what if you linger while others race by,
Holding back as they reach for the sky?
Don't fear defeat or the sting of loss,
For rushing through life comes at a cost..

There's a curious rush in the drive to succeed,
It makes you overlook the blessings you need.
At times, it breeds envy and frustration's
sway,
Comparing your path to others, you lose your
way.

But here's the remedy for that endless chase,
Find satisfaction—embrace your own pace.:
Let envy spark self-improvement's fire,
A drive for growth and dreams to aspire..

So run your race, but find your own stride,
Let envy inspire you, with grace as your guide.
In this journey of life, it's clear,
Success is sweetest when it's truly yours, dear..

I pledge to you

Let me recount the moments that wove you
into my life's tale,
A vivid slideshow of glory, where love will
never pale.

From vowing our lives to one another's
embrace,
to overcoming every challenge that we face.

It feels as if destiny wove a grand design,
A tapestry of moments that only hearts can
define.

Now, as we stand together, my love, here's my pledge to you,
A vow of endless devotion, pure and true.

I pledge my life to you beneath the endless sky,
I pledge my soul, with every breath and sigh.

I pledge my highs and lows, my deepest emotion,
I pledge my strength and boundless devotion..

Through every twist and turn, wherever life may lead,
I pledge to stand by you in every moment and need..

My Family Celebrates me

Let me tell you a little secret, I'm truly blessed,
My family embraces me, my flaws and all, and loves me best.

My mom cheers my culinary trials, even when they're amiss,
My dad applauds my choices, even those I'd like to dismiss.
All my mindless decisions have taught me a lesson, he says..
Life teaches you lessons in its own unique ways.

My brother, so patient, endures my whimsical sway,
He says, "With you, chaos and vigilance find their way."

My husband celebrates me when I feel less than bright,
He says my imperfections make me shine more bright.

Indeed, I'm fortunate, with family so dear,
Their love lifts my spirit and makes my path clear.

In their unwavering support, I find my true might,
Blessed with their love, I embrace myself with delight.

Wanderlust

Gazing through a café window, in a place unknown,
A profound thought struck me, like a stone sharply thrown.
We race through our days from dawn until night,
Chasing after luxuries and societal delight.

While many feed their bodies,
I choose to fodder my soul.
Life's essence resides in moments, experiences untold,
Happiness, my true quest, a treasure chest to unfold.

I choose to wander, to become nameless,
unseen,
Leaving only memories, evoking emotions,
serene.

Every journey reshapes me and makes me feel
most alive.
As I set foot on a foreign land, I am reborn, a
lass, and alive.

It will never be enough!!

Let me tell you a story of a miss who went
into the countryside to relax,
There was greenery everywhere—something
magical in those wild tracks..

Looking through the car window, she was
creating her own fairy-tale,
Through her inquisitive eyes, she found
perfection in the imperfect trees and their
pale, fading leaves..

After driving a few miles, she saw a village wanderer with his sheep.
He was a man in his mid-sixties; his beard was grey, and his voice heavy and deep.

The greybeard struck up a conversation as he noticed her admiring the place.
The girl appreciated the beauty of the place and said that he was lucky to stay there.
The man seemed unconvinced and asked, 'Is it really so idyllic to live in the middle of nowhere?"

IIt was clear the greybeard favored the chaos of urban streets,
And the girl wondered how someone could prefer the concrete jungle over the peace of trees.

Each believed the other was living the better life,
Yet both overlooked the adversities they each had to survive.

For everyone out there, some part of this ride called life is rough.
For each one of us, it will absolutely never be enough.

Rainfall

Aaahh! Here come the clouds,
I gaze at these dusky spheres from my
window, far from the bustling crowd..

On a rainy day, a cozy blanket I take,
Hot coffee in hand and a book — my perfect
nook..
Rain's rhythm and tempo, as tranquil as a
brook.

While most seek the sun's radiant ray,
I find solace in the rain, come what may.

Little droplets fall, cleansing the ground,
Washing away past sorrows, summer's heat
unbound.

Rain purifies, with each droplet's descent,
Breathing life into tales, where new stories are sent.

I wish, as it cleanses the earth's worldly goals,
It could also purify hearts and mend fractured souls.

Swimming against the current

Trust yourself and embrace the fall,
Fear's grip can crumble when you stand tall.

Dive into the waters, feel the deep current's grace,
Let go, surrender, let faith set the pace.

Having faith is like surrendering to the flow,
Soft and supple, yet it can wear you down slow.

Don't try to grip it, or you'll surely descend,
Relax, release, and you'll ascend without end.

Love allows for disagreements

When roadblocks rise between hearts so near,
In love's embrace, respect we hold dear.

Disagreements, they come, then fade away,
Yet emotions, at times, lead us astray.

In moments of folly, when reason takes flight,
How can we bridge the gap, find common
light?

Misunderstandings obscure the view,
But an open heart can restore the hue.

Opposition may seem naive or unkind,
Yet beneath the surface, treasures we find.

Dig deep, my love, and you shall uncover,
The roots of beliefs we'd often smother. .

Amid grievances voiced and complaints laid bare,
Our shared quest for joy shows how much we care.

In this dance of love, where two souls engage,
Blame fades away as we turn a new page.

For love is the compass that guides us true,
Together we'll learn, we'll grow, we'll renew.

Stand up for each other ladies!

If not us, then who else will understand the
pain,
Who'll comprehend the depths of a woman's
mind?

We all know the sting of being seen as
vulnerable,,
The constant sense of being perceived as
weak.
To have our emotions respected—validation
many of us seek..

The perpetual juggle of our multifaceted roles,
Daughter, mother, wife, sister – we're eternal superheroes with life's goals.

So much is expected of us by society.
Each one of us is told how to dress, how to walk, how to behave..
At every point in life there is someone out there judging and ready to instruct.

But times, they are changing, and I truly believe,
That women are achieving greatness—oh, what we can conceive!

Let's celebrate their victories, hard-won and bright,
For each battle they've fought, for every challenging fight.

We have struggled and learnt to raise our voice.
May this fire within us always burn bright,
however small or concealed.
May this fire within us always burn bright!

Thank You!!!

A new chapter begins,
And I never thought it would be this smooth..
You arrived like a beacon,
transforming my life's groove.

Disappointments and betrayals had me confined,
But you proved life's twists and turns can be realigned.

Embracing the chaos, bidding the past adieu,
You offered me forgiveness, so genuine and true.

You're like sunlight breaking through the cloudy veil,
Radiating warmth, revealing life's wondrous tale.

My once aimless path, void of zeal and cheer,
Now blooms with passion, profoundly sincere.
This verdant journey casts away all my doubt,
With you, insecurities dissolve—no room for doubt. .

I cherish this journey we share,
My mind rests easy, free from despair.

I wonder, where were you in days of old,
When I needed your warmth and embrace to hold?

I've found my place, it's where I've always belonged,
Thank you, my love, for making everything clear and strong.

For mending what was broken, for your
gentle grace,
Gratitude fills my heart, an unspoken
embrace.

Thank you, with all my heart's full light,,
For being my guiding star, my beacon of light.

Clay

I observed a potter, shaping clay with artful play,
Their hands—a dance of skill and grace upon the pliant clay..
With patience and precision, they worked the earth so fine,
They created wonders from their soul, each piece a grand design.

Inspired by their art, I took my turn in kind,
Imagining a form unique, with thoughts that intertwined.
But soon I learned the subtle truth of this creative art,
A balance delicate as a whisper, a dance of hand and heart.

For with a heavy-handed touch, the clay
began to strain,
Its shape contorted, spirit lost, as I learned
from the pain.
Yet in that moment of mistake, a lesson came
to light,
To cherish every tender stroke, to create with
love and sight.

So, as I shaped my clay anew, I vowed to
softly mold,
With devotion to the craft, as each story was
retold..
For in the clay, I found a truth, a lesson to
embrace,
That beauty lies in gentleness, in artful,
tender grace.

Teardrops

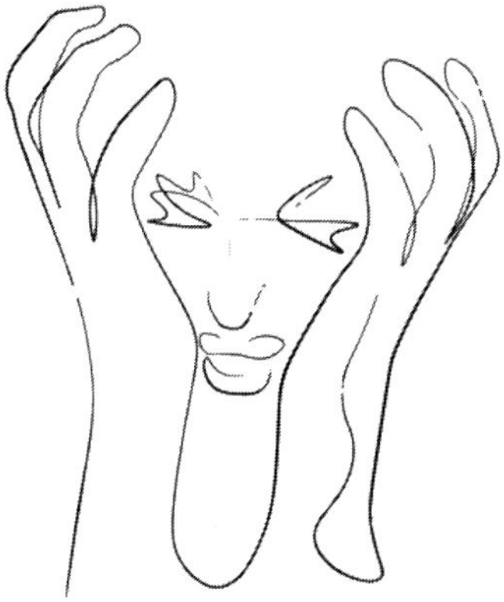

When tears grace your cheek,
Don't see them as frailty or a reflection of weakness.
See them as the essence of your soul's gentle strength—
Each warm, salty drop, a balm for inner strife,
Mending the heart's fissures with their healing light.

In those teardrops, find the strength to restore,
As they wash away the dust from your sight once more,
Bringing clarity to the world, pure and bright,
Let each tear be your guide through the darkest night.

When a lump forms in your throat, do not fear,
For in that lump lies courage—let it flow, my dear.
It'll cleanse your soul, wash away the pain,
And in its soothing embrace, you'll find peace again.

I choose you!

I choose you over everything else,
When I gaze through these eyes, my heart melts,

I choose you when you protect all my sanity with your madness,
I choose you when my despair becomes your sadness.

I'll choose you, even if you step away from my side,
Through truth and through lies, in you, I confide.

Even if you wound me, tearing at my core,
I'll choose you forever, that's a promise I
swore.

In the boundless realm of love, they say we're
blind,
I'll choose you, my dear,till the end of time. .

Comparisons

Comparing your life to others — a futile quest,,
Like dismissing your breath while you're alive and blessed.

Measuring your worth by another's pace,
Neglects the beauty of your unique grace.

Each one has their path, their share of good and bad,
Comparison, a thief of joy, leaves you feeling sad.

My friend, you're a star on your own
journey's flight,
Embrace your uniqueness, for in it, you shine
so bright.

Even if you see others succeed and shine,
Remember, your own story is one of a kind,
your story is yours to author and revise. .

You are here only for a while!

Don't forget that you are here for a while,
This journey will end, and you will flee to a
new dimension leaving everything behind..
So, live this moment,
take risks and smile.
Remember, you are here only for a while.

Craft memories, yearn for wonders.
Believe me, I've witnessed miracles unfold.
I've seen trees sprout from the heart of stone.

Your life is like a blank canvas,
Splash it with the hues of your own choosing,
Embrace the shades of your mistakes,
achievements, and regrets,
For each color is beautiful — a testament to
your own creation.
Whatever you do, etch this in your heart,
you are here only for a while.

The Cycle of Life

A strange emotion — seeing your parents age,
,
In life's quiet unfolding, this is an emotional stage.

The hands that held you, guided you, shaped you, ,
now seek support,
They term it 'the cycle of life' — a sad retort. .

As wrinkles deepen on their foreheads, a masterpiece of time's own chart,
Aches echo within the chambers of my heart.
I desire to smooth those lines with a tender art,
But reality whispers, erasure plays no part.

Still, the hands that shaped me remain my heroes,
Their physical vigour may decline, but mental strength only grows.
Guiding and inspiring with a resilient glow,
In their presence, I find safety, and love continues to sow. .

Rising not Falling in Love

They say love makes you fall, but I defy.
For I have not fallen, instead, I've soared high.
In your love, I found wings to take flight,
To chart my course amidst the starry night.

Your love, a gentle breeze beneath my wings,
Guiding me through life's uncertain springs.
No falling here, just rising high,
In your embrace, I reach for the sky.
With your love, I shape my destiny's grace,
Empowered by your embrace.

So let them speak of falls and lows,
But with you, my heart always grows,
With your love, I rise and soar,
Forever thankful for what's in store.

All my "What ifs"

In moments, I ponder: what if your heart chose someone new,
Would she make you smile brighter — or maybe just a little less blue?
Would you argue softly, or with a heated fight?
And in her eyes, would you see sparks like ours ignite?

I worry about silly things, like fights over the mundane,
These thoughts bother me, causing aches and pain.
I wonder if she'd bring you more joy and delight,
Yet deep down, my love for you still takes flight.

But amidst this doubt, your embrace brings me peace,
In your arms, my worries find a gentle release.
Though uncertainties linger, our love remains true —
Through all the "what ifs," I choose to stand by you.

Connected Across Distance

Can you believe it? Even when apart,
We breathe the same air, under one vast sky's art.
The moon we gaze upon, its light knows no divide,
Binding us in thought, across the distance wide.

With every breath I take, you're close in my heart,
Joined by stars above, never truly apart.

The Balloon Seller's Lesson

Today, at the traffic lights,
I saw a young boy with bright eyes,
His hair unkempt, his skin dark and worn,
A face unwashed, yet his eyes twinkled with life.
In his small hands, he held balloons,
Bright and colorful, a splash of joy,
He was selling them at the busy lights,
His face carried an innocence untouched by the world.
He approached me with a gentle smile,
"Would you like a balloon?" he asked.

I glanced at him and said,
"What will I do with them?"
He nodded, his smile unbroken,
And moved on to the next car.
Through my rearview mirror, I watched him,
Something about his innocence drew me in.
I called him back, wanting to help,
Offered him money, saying,
"I don't need the balloon."
He smiled again, this time with a depth that stung my heart.
"Thank you, *didi*," he said,
"But I'm not a beggar."
His words struck me like a wave,
That little boy taught me a lesson for life.
In his quiet refusal, I learned of dignity in hardship,
That true strength lies in holding onto self-respect,
Even when life is harsh and the world offers pity.
And I realized the misconception of kindness—
It's not in the money given, but in the respect shown,

For kindness without dignity is a gift unreceived,
And in his eyes, I saw the power of earning one's keep,
A lesson that will forever resonate within me.

My Father Sends Me Memories

Today, my phone chimed softly,
A message from Dad—
A picture of my younger self,
Wide-eyed, with a mischievous grin.
It's something he does now,
Ever since I left home,
To find my own path,
To carve out a life on my own.
He opens those old albums,
Dusty with years gone by,
And sends me snapshots of a time
When life was simpler,
When we were small,
And he was our world.
I think he misses those days,

When we depended on him,
When our small hands reached out
For candies and car rides,
When he was our hero,
Our guide through the unknown.
Now, with each photo sent,
I feel his longing across the distance,
A quiet reminder that home
Is where we first learned to dream,
Where we were once his little ones,
Tugging at his sleeve,
Trusting him to lead the way.
I know he misses us,
The sound of our laughter filling the halls,
The warmth of our presence,
The way we made the house a home.
And though we've grown and gone,
Carrying pieces of him wherever we roam,
In each photo, I see his heart,
Holding on to the days when we were his,
And he was the center of our small universe.

When I Cry Before You

When I cry before you,
It means I trust you enough
To lay my heart bare,
To show you the cracks,
The places where I'm fragile,
Where the world has left its mark.

In those moments, I am vulnerable,
Unraveled — like a thread undone —
But I trust you to hold me,
To see me as I am.

When you wipe my tears
With your soft, gentle palms,
It's more than just comfort—
It's a promise unspoken,
That you'll stand beside me
In my sorrow and my joy,
That my tears are safe with you,
That my heart is in good hands.

So, when I cry before you,
Know it's because I trust you,
With the parts of me that tremble,
With the pieces that sometimes break.
And when you wipe my tears,
I know I'm not alone —
For in your touch, I find a home
Where my heart can always return.

The Wonder Within

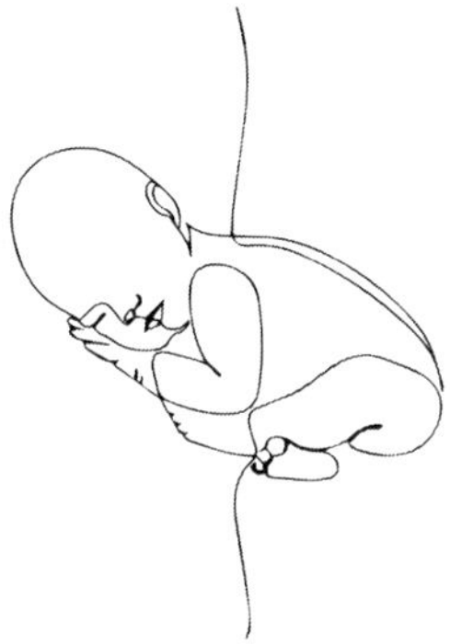

I can't help but wonder—
How does a woman create life within her?
How am I doing this?
It amazes me to think
That right now, inside me,
Something incredible is happening.
I find myself asking,
Which part of me is working tirelessly,
Day and night,
To form those tiny hands,
Those little legs,
And that soft, new skin?
I've heard people talk about this magic,
But now that it's happening to me,
Now that I can feel it,

I'm in awe of my own body,
Of what it can do without me even knowing how.
There's this energy inside me,
Something deep and powerful,
That just knows how to create,
How to shape life in the quiet,
How to do this beautiful work
— that I can't see, but can feel growing every day..
I find myself respecting my body more,
Appreciating the way it just knows,
The way it becomes a creator,
Almost like it has its own wisdom,
A knowledge that's as old as time.
And the magic of it all—
It truly blows me away.
I'm carrying this little miracle inside me,
A part of the infinite,
And it fills me with wonder every single day.

In the Silence of Strength

In the silence of night, when the world lies still,
A soft prayer escapes, a whisper, a will.
For my brother, out there in his uniform,
Brave and strong, weathering every storm.

They say we're strong, that we bear the weight,
But they don't see the fear we often debate.
Each badge and star makes our hearts swell,
But behind the pride, there's a worry we quell.

Yes, we're proud—how could we not be?
Yet every day, fear tugs silently.
We wrestle with thoughts, with shadows and doubt,
And in every prayer, we pour our love out.

They say we're unbreakable, tough as steel,
But inside, we tremble—we fear, we feel.
Families of soldiers—they call us strong,
But we're just trying to hold on all along.

We stand by our heroes, proud and tall,
But we're human too, and that says it all.
In every heartbeat, in every sigh,
There's a prayer for his safety, a tear in our eye.

So yes, we're strong, but we're also afraid,
In the quiet of the night, where memories are made.
We love, we worry, we hope, we pray,
And we carry on, day by day.

Winner in My Stories

My mind is a strange place — it twists, and it bends.
When I feel like I've failed, it rewrites my ends.
I sit in my thoughts, replaying the day,
Changing my choices, imagining a new way.

In those moments of doubt, I become the hero,
Turning my losses into stories of growth.
It's how I cope with the pain I can't shake,
Finding strength in my heart, for my own sake.

Though the world may see me as less than I'd like,
In my mind, I stand tall, ready to strike.
For in the quiet of thought, I learn to believe,
That even in struggle, I'm stronger than grief.

Love's Power

Love is stronger than we know,
A force that whispers, then grows.
It shapes the soul, it lifts the heart,
Transforming us right from the very start.
It can make you whole, make you new,
A mirror reflecting a different view,
From the depths of your very core,
Love opens doors you hadn't seen before.
For love is not just soft and sweet,
It's a power that none can beat,
A force that moves, that molds, that bends,
Changing us from start to end.

Stronger than the storms of time,
It lifts us up, makes us climb,
Love is a journey, a quiet guide,
It turns our worlds from dark to light.
In its embrace, we are reborn,
Love, a fire that makes us warm,
And in its grasp, we find our wings,
A new life, where hope begins.

Seeing Beyond Judgement

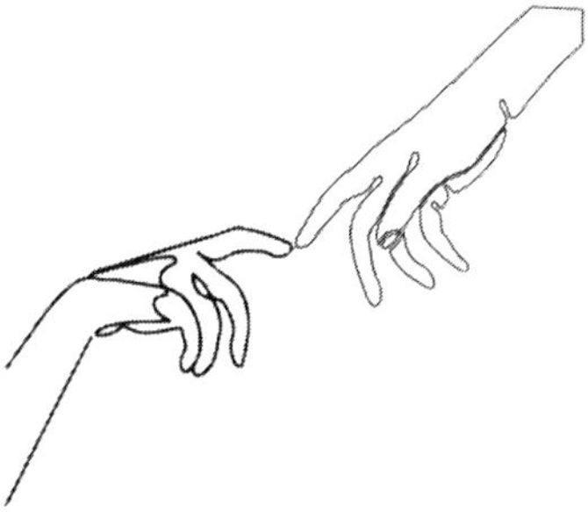

The other day, as I drove along,
An old man came, his voice so strong,
A Sikh, just like me, with hands so frail,
He asked for some money, his face worn pale.

In our Sikh belief, we're taught to stand,
To work with honor, to lend a hand.
Begging is not the path we strive to take — ,
We're taught to earn, not for others' sake.
Yet, seeing his age, .I gave him a bit —
Not a lot, just enough to fit.
And as I started to drive away,
Something caught my eye, something I
couldn't sway.

I saw him go to his wife so dear,
And hand her the money, with love sincere.
Maybe they truly needed it, I thought,
Perhaps that was all they had, all they sought.
In that moment, I felt a shift,
My heart grew heavy, my mind adrift.
I had judged too quickly, too harshly, I see —
What if I'd given more, what could it be?
Had I let my thoughts be clouded and blind,
When kindness was all I needed to find?
Now I know, it's not for me to decide,
How others live, or what they hide.
Sometimes the lessons come too late,
But today, I learned—don't judge, just relate.

Love Like Water

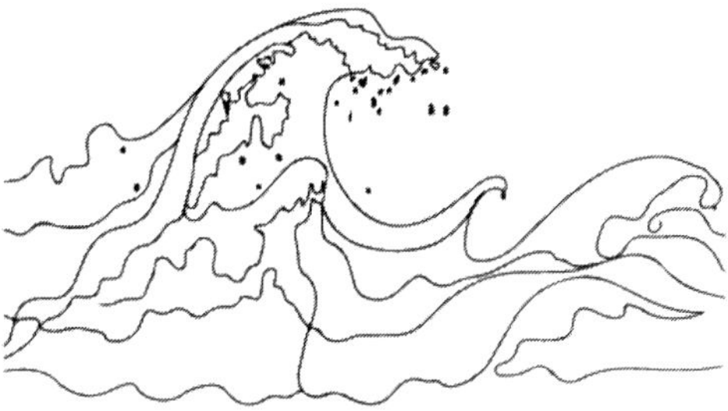

Your love is like water, calm and kind,
It cools my anger, it eases my mind.
When anger blazes or frustration ignites,
You flow through my soul, calming the fights.
In moments I crave, longing and bare,
You drench my heart with tender care.
Like water takes the shape it's poured into,
Your love fits my feelings, steady and true.
It knows my contours, my highs and my lows,
Quenching the embers where warmth softly glows.
Your love, like water, steady and true,
Brings life, brings peace, and sees me through.